Alice H. Parker

and the Furnace

By Virginia Loh-Hagan

21st Century
Junior Library

Published in the United States of America by
Cherry Lake Publishing
Ann Arbor, Michigan
www.cherrylakepublishing.com

Content Adviser: Kirsten Edwards, MA, Educational Studies
Reading Adviser: Marla Conn, MS, Ed., Literacy specialist, Read-Ability, Inc.

Photo Credits: © Olivier Le Moal/Shutterstock.com, Cover, 1; © LightField Studios/Shutterstock.com, 4; ©12019/
Pixabay.com, 6; LBJ Library photo by Yoichi Okamoto/Serial No. A1030-8a/Public Domain/LBJ Library, 8; ©Harry Green/
Shutterstock.com, 10; ©Alice H. Parker (US1325905-1)/United States Patent and Trademark Office/www.uspto.gov,
12; © Toonzzz/Shutterstock.com, 14; © JaySi/Shutterstock.com, 16; © Andrey_Popov/Shutterstock.com, 18; © PointImages/
Shutterstock.com, 20

Library of Congress Cataloging-in-Publication Data has been filed and is available at catalog.loc.gov

Cherry Lake Publishing would like to acknowledge the work of The Partnership for 21st Century Skills.
Please visit *www.p21.org* for more information.

Printed in the United States of America
Corporate Graphics

CONTENTS

Inventors make life easier for us.

A Woman

What do you do when you get cold? What do you do when you get hot? Today, you can change the room **temperature**. You can heat up or cool down a room. You don't have to do much to make this happen. You turn a dial or you flip a switch. This is because of Alice H. Parker.

Parker was an African American woman. She invented a special **furnace**. Furnaces heat homes and buildings.

Howard University has provided higher education to African Americans since 1866.

Parker lived in Morristown, New Jersey. Around 1910, she studied at Howard University. She was a great student. She earned top grades in her classes. She earned a **certificate**.

Howard University is a special school. It is in Washington, D.C., which is the nation's capital. It was one of the few schools that

Create!

Create your own invention. Parker added to what she already knew about furnaces. She made them better. Think about something you use every day. How can you make it better?

African Americans didn't get the right to vote until 1965.

taught black students. It also taught women. It was difficult for both these groups to have higher education during that time.

During Parker's life, few African Americans were educated. Even fewer African American women were educated. Black women faced many challenges. They were not treated fairly. They were not given the same opportunities.

Parker was highly educated for her time. But she had to work extra hard. She had to fight against **racism**. She also fought against **sexism**. She didn't quit.

Furnace systems have been around since ancient Rome.

An Idea

Morristown gets cold in the winter. Parker was tired of being cold. She had to rely on fireplaces to make heat. Fireplaces were limited. They didn't heat up the whole house. They were also a lot of work. People had to chop wood to build the fires. They had to watch the fires. It was unsafe to leave it unattended. Fireplaces were also messy. The smoke from the fireplace would

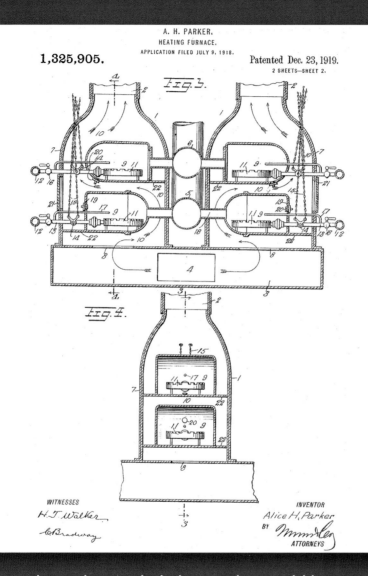

Parker's plans included **vents** that could be moved.

sometimes fill the house. Fireplaces also left ash. It went everywhere.

Parker saw an opportunity. She wanted to make life better. She wanted to make life easier. She designed a heating furnace. She got a **patent** on December 23, 1919.

Other people had invented furnaces. But Parker improved their designs. She used gas to power the furnace. This got rid of the need for coal or wood. She designed air **ducts**. These ducts delivered heat to different parts of the building.

Parker's design also saved energy. She came up with a way to control heat. Hot air could move to different rooms by using

Inventors build on each other's ideas.

multiple **burners**. All of this was managed by a switch. People could have more control over temperatures.

Her design wasn't ready to be built. There were safety issues with the heat flow. But her idea led to many more important ideas. Other inventors used her ideas.

Think!

Imagine a time before furnaces. Think about what you would do. Could you chop wood every day? Could you tend a fire all day long? What would your life be like?

Parker's idea reduced the danger of fire
caused by fireplaces.

A Legacy

Parker was the first to think of **central heating**. Her ideas led to safer systems. Millions of homes and buildings around the world have central heating. This is because of Parker.

Her ideas led to the invention of the **thermostat** and to **forced-air** furnaces. Her **legacy** can be seen in modern living. She changed how people live. People no longer had to tend fires.

Even today, getting patents is not an easy process.

Parker also paved the way for others. She was a role model for African American women inventors. Not many African Americans or women could get patents at this time. But Parker was successful.

There weren't many jobs open to black women then. Many worked in homes as maids. Parker opened up opportunities. She wanted everyone to have better lives.

Parker's ideas had a great impact on the world. In 2014, the New Jersey **Chamber of Commerce** honored her.

We may not know what Parker looks like, but we do know she made winters a little warmer.

They named her a "Top Innovator from New Jersey." They named the award after her.

Sadly, not much is known about Parker. Her life is a mystery. Her patent is the only clue we have about her work. We're lucky to have her patent. Think about Parker on cold nights!

Make a Guess!

The only record we have of Parker is her patent. Guess why we don't know much about Parker. Think about how we learn about other famous people. What makes Parker different from others?

GLOSSARY

burners (BUR-nurz) tools in a furnace that burn fuel to heat air

central heating (SEN-truhl HEE-ting) a system for heating buildings by heating air in one place and sending it through the whole building

certificate (sur-TIF-uh-kit) a piece of paper that states something is a fact

chamber of commerce (CHAYM-bur OV KAH-murs) a local group that promotes businesses

ducts (DUHKTS) channels or tubes that move things from one place to another

forced-air (FORSD-air) a heating system that distributes heat throughout a building using air to carry it

furnace (FUR-nis) an enclosed container that makes heat

legacy (LEG-uh-see) something handed down from one generation to another

patent (PAT-uhnt) the right from the government to use or sell an invention for a certain number of years

racism (RAY-siz-uhm) the unfair treatment of people from certain groups based on the belief that one race is better than the others

sexism (SEX-iz-uhm) the unfair treatment of women or men based on the belief that one gender is better than the other

temperature (TEM-pur-uh-chur) a measure of warmth or coldness

thermostat (THUR-muh-stat) a device that controls temperature

vents (VENTS) openings that allow heat to escape

FIND OUT MORE

BOOKS

Abdul-Jabbar, Kareem, and Raymond Obstfeld. *What Color Is My World? The Lost History of African-American Inventors*. Somerville, MA: Candlewick Press, 2012.

Lawrence, Sarah. *Anthology of Amazing Women: Trailblazers Who Dared to Be Different*. New York: Little Bee Books, 2018.

Sullivan, Otha Richard. *Black Stars: African American Women Scientists and Inventors*. San Francisco: Jossey-Bass, 2012.

WEBSITES

New Jersey Chamber of Commerce: The Fascinating Story of Alice H. Parker
http://newjerseycc.com/galaguide/top25/15-20-alice-h-parker
Learn more about what is known about Alice H. Parker's life and accomplishments.

Yes! Magazine: 10 Black Women Innovators and the Awesome Things They Brought Us
www.yesmagazine.org/happiness/10-black-women-innovators-and-the-awesome-things-they-brought-us-20160321
Read about Alice H. Parker and nine other women innovators and their inventions.

INDEX

ABOUT THE AUTHOR

Dr. Virginia Loh-Hagan is an author, university professor, former classroom teacher, and curriculum designer. She's very thankful for central air and heating. She can't chop wood. She lives in San Diego with her very tall husband and very naughty dogs. To learn more about her, visit www.virginialoh.com.